DURHAM
CATHEDRAL

D0690189

Contents

Left: ①
Replica of the
Sanctuary Knocker.
Clinging to this
knocker criminals
might claim sanctuary
in the cathedral until
their offences had
been pardoned by the
king. The original is in
the Cathedral Treasury.

History Chart

998 "The White Church" dedicated by monks from Lindisfarne to shelter St. Cuthbert's body.

1022 Bede's remains removed from Jarrow and brought to Durham.

1093 Foundations of present cathedral laid by Bishop William and the Benedictine monks.

1093–1133 Choir, Transepts and Nave built with stone-vaulted roofs.

1133–40 Chapter House built.

1175–89 Galilee Chapel built.

1242–74 Chapel of the Nine Altars built.

1372–80 Neville Screen built.

1465–90 Bell Tower rebuilt.

1541 Henry VIII reconstituted the church as the Cathedral Church of Christ and Blessed Mary the Virgin.

1626–72 Beautification of Cathedral by Dean Hunt and Bishop Cosin.

1650 Destruction of many medieval wooden furnishings by Cromwell's prisoners after the Battle of Dunbar.

1777 Urgent repairs to cracks in the vaulting and bulging walls.

1832 University founded by Bishop van Mildert and the Cathedral Chapter.

1870–6 Choir screen and alabaster pulpit designed and built by Gilbert Scott.

1895 Chapter House restored in memory of Bishop Lightfoot.

1980 Bells rehung in steel frame.

1980 30-year restoration of stonework begun by Cathedral masons.

1984–5 North and south door lobbies designed by Ian Curry, made by Cathedral craftsmen.

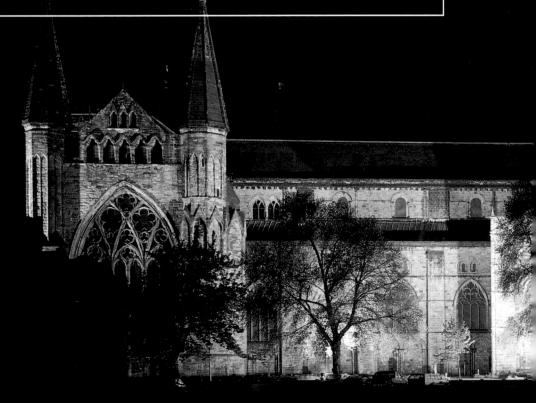

Welcome to Durham Cathedral!

First sight of it, from the train or from Palace Green, is breath-taking. Equally breath-taking, when you enter, is the impact of carved stone pillars, strength and stay of the whole amazing edifice. A triumph of engineering. A creation of faith. A parable of God.

There would have been no Cathedral, had it not been for Cuthbert of Lindisfarne, best loved saint of the north-east. His mortal remains found their last resting-place here in Durham and now lie under a plain marble slab behind the high altar. The richly ornamented medieval shrine is destroyed, but his spirit is alive, and folk still gather at his tomb to join their prayers with his.

Those of us who live and work in and around the Cathedral are part of this living tradition. A 'community of care-takers', we look after the buildings, encourage learning and the arts, welcome visitors. But the heart of our business is the daily worship offered to God on behalf of God's whole world.

We warmly welcome our twentieth-century visitors and pilgrims to 'Cuthbert's Church'. Our prayer is that in coming to Durham Cathedral you will feel you have 'come home', and that when you leave you will go on your way rejoicing.

THE DEAN

St. Cuthbert and the Venerable Bede

Left: (14)
The tester, designed by Sir Ninian Comper, above St. Cuthbert's tomb.

Below: (14)
The Tomb of St. Cuthbert. The remains of the Saint still rest beneath this grey stone slab on the site of his ancient shrine.

St. Cuthbert

Durham Cathedral would never h[ave] existed had it not been for St. Cuthber[t. It] was built as a shrine for this famous a[nd] best loved saint of the north-east. A[s a] shepherd boy on the hills of Lamm[er]moor, Cuthbert had seen in a vis[ion] the soul of St. Aidan being carrie[d to] heaven by the hands of angels, and, t[hus] inspired, had become a monk. Thou[gh] he himself would have preferred the [life] of a hermit, his reputation for sanc[tity] and learning became so great that [the] people insisted he should be mad[e a] bishop, and he was consecrated Bis[hop] of Lindisfarne in 685. Two years late[r he] died on Farne Island and was burie[d in] the church at Lindisfarne. Ten ye[ars] after his death his body was found t[o be] without signs of decay and was place[d in] a shrine above ground level.

There it rested for 200 years u[ntil] Danish raids made it wise for the mo[nks] to seek safety elsewhere. St. Cuth[bert] had ordered that if ever they left Lin[dis]farne, the monks should take his bo[dy] with them; so his shrine was opened [and] to their astonishment and awe his b[ody] still appeared as free from decay as [on] the day when it was buried. They [re]closed it in a wooden coffin, and, tak[ing] it with them, began the wanderi[ngs] which lasted until AD 995, when t[hey] finally discovered a place of safety o[n a] rocky piece of land almost entirely s[ur]rounded by the River Wear. Here t[hey] sheltered the Saint's body for a time [in a] little church made of the boughs of tr[ees] while they began to build someth[ing] better.

The new building was called "[The] White Church" and it remained [the] shrine of St. Cuthbert until it was pu[lled] down in 1092, to make way for a [new] cathedral. Until 1104 the body of [St.] Cuthbert was protected in a tempor[ary] shrine, but in 1104 the shrine beh[ind] the High Altar was ready. The mo[nks]

had prepared everything for the removal of the precious relic, but on the night before this was due to happen the heavy timbering which supported the vault over the new tomb was still in place and taking it down promised to be a difficult task; "but," says the chronicler, "on the morning of the day itself this was all found lying flat on the ground with nothing harmed"; it was claimed that the Saint himself had brought about its fall.

In about 1140, Bishop de Puiset began to erect a Lady Chapel at the east end of the cathedral, but the walls were not many yards above the ground when they began to show cracks and it was argued that St. Cuthbert did not want to have such a chapel so near his tomb. The Bishop stopped building there and moved his men and materials to the west end where about 1175 he erected the present Galilee Chapel.

The shrine of St. Cuthbert was the Cathedral's great glory and a chief centre of pilgrimage. Kings and prelates came there and multitudes of lesser people, bringing their offerings and their prayers. Men might approach the Saint's shrine, but women were never allowed to do so. There is a line of black Frosterley marble stretching across the floor just in front of the font, and beyond this women

Left: (19)
Peter the Deacon. Embroidered 10th-century stole given to the shrine of St. Cuthbert.

Below: (19)
The remains of St. Cuthbert's coffin, made for the Saint's body in 698.

Right: ④
Bede's tomb still holds the Saint's remains, placed there in 1370. Up to that time they were in St. Cuthbert's shrine.

Right (inset): ③
The Galilee Chapel, which probably got its name because it was the last stage of the Sunday Great Procession, which symbolised Our Lord's return to Galilee.

Below: ⑲
The Pectoral Cross taken from St. Cuthbert's coffin in 1827. It is 7th-century Northumbrian work, of gold cloisonné.

were not allowed to go. In 1333 Queen Philippa, the wife of King Edward III, was staying in Durham, in the Prior's lodgings. She was roused in the middle of the night, told of the Saint's supposed dislike of women and offered a bed in the castle. The Queen got up and, in reverence of the Saint, instead of taking the direct way through the cathedral, she went out through the great gate of the monastery, past the east end of the cathedral and along Dun Cow Lane to the castle, entreating the saint not to avenge a fault which she had committed in ignorance.

There are three separate lists of the treasures which accumulated at St. Cuthbert's shrine. Among them are some very extraordinary claims. There was a part of the rod of Moses, a piece of the manger of Our Lord, a piece of the tree under which were the three Angels with Abraham, a piece of the throne of the twelve Apostles, a mass of garments supposed to have belonged to a great number of saints and an equally great number of portions of their bodies. There was the claw of a griffin and several griffin's eggs, together with a great number of caskets in ivory, and crystal; cups, crosses and jewels of gold set with precious stones – a vast heap of treasure. The shrine itself, says the *Rites of Durham*, "was estimated to be one of the most sumptuous monuments in all England, so great were the offerings and jewels bestowed upon it, and endless the miracles that were wrought at it, even in these later days." On 31st December 1540, the monastery of Durham was surrendered to the Crown and its riches confiscated. In particular there was, belonging to St. Cuthbert's shrine, a precious stone which the jewellers said was worth "a King's ransom". When the shrine itself was broken open the body of the Saint was found lying on its side

"whole, incorrupt, with his face b and his beard as it had been, a fortnig growth, and all his vestments upon I as he had been accustomed to say M withall."

The coffin had been opened at vari times in the Middle Ages and some of vestments changed. The body on ev occasion was reported to be incorru For a time it was kept reverently in vestry until the King's pleasure migh known. Finally, it was buried unde plain marble slab on the spot where shrine had stood; there it still remair

The Venerable Bede
In addition to the bones of St. Cuthb the monastic building at Durham a possessed the bones of the Venera Bede. That scholarly Saint, who refu the honour of becoming abbot of monastery at Jarrow in order to pur his scholastic work, was author of *Church History of the English Peo* which has perpetuated his name. died and was buried at Jarrow in 7 but about the year 1022 a monk ca Aelfred stole the remains and brou them to Durham, where he was a sac and added them to the collection of re of Northern Saints which he had alre accumulated. The ancient monaste of St. Peter, Monkwearmouth, and Paul, Jarrow, where the Venerable B had lived and worked, had alre begun a renewed life with monks fr the south who kept the Benedictine strictly. Bishop William brought th men to Durham to be the nucleu a community there, and so Durh became the heir to the two houses wh in the days of Benedict Biscop and B had been the cradle of English learni

Durham Cathedral is unique. It is the finest example of Early Norman architecture in England and its massive grandeur is enhanced by the magnificence of the site.

After the Conquest in 1066 the Normans turned their attention to the north. The castle at Durham was begun in 1071, at a time when most of the north of England was beyond the rule of law. A Norman settlement needed to be established that could withstand the savage attacks of the Scots and the fiercely independent borderers. (Durham was the only major city near the border to resist capture by the Scots.)

In 1080 William the Conqueror granted palatine, or royal, powers to the Prince Bishop of Durham, William of St. Calais. He was expected to be a religious and a military leader, and to exercise directly many of the King's own powers – a unique position for a baron in England at that time.

There was already a religious community in Durham dating back to 998, when "the White Church" was dedicated by Saxon Benedictine monks as a burial place for St. Cuthbert. The second Norman bishop, William of St. Calais (1081–96), was the founder, in 1093, of the present cathedral.

In 1088 William of St. Calais was accused of having plotted against William Rufus, and was exiled to Normandy. He returned to Durham in 1091, and in the next year destroyed the Saxon church completely in preparation for his own building. In 1093, on 11th August, the foundations of the present cathedral were laid by Bishop William, Prior Turgot, and the brethren.

The bishopric passed, in 1099, to another highly political bishop, Ranulph Flambard, who was skilful at political intrigue and raising tax revenue for the King. He found the choir and the crossing already completed. In 1104, the

All this was done by 1133. In forty yea and under two bishops the cathedi which William of St. Calais had plann was completed. It stands today vast a impressive in its massive strength, a yet so well-proportioned that there nothing about it that seems pondero Together with the Norman castle whi guarded the neck of the peninsula, made a fortress which was impregna before the days of cannon. Part of interior of the cathedral was decora in red and black. A small portion of pattern can be seen on the south arca ing near the Neville Tomb.

Building still went on. The chap house was erected by Geoffrey Ru (1113–40). Hugh de Puiset, the neph of that strong-minded woman, Que Matilda, obtained the bishopric at powerful aunt's insistence and in face of much local opposition. He ju fied his appointment, however, for was a noble builder, though his arc tects seem to have been better arti than engineers. He began the building the Galilee Chapel.

The stone columns of the Gali Chapel were added by Thomas Langl Bishop of Durham (1406–37) a cardi and twice Chancellor of England. He a built the great buttresses on the outs of the west walls, which prevent building from slipping into the river, de Puiset's architect could not be bo ered with foundations and sank the b of his pillars hardly more than a foot two below the ground. Cardinal Lang completed his work on the Gali Chapel by building his own tomb wit it, in front of the west door of the gr church.

In 1228 Richard le Poore, author the *Ancren Riwle*, was translated fr Salisbury, where he had erected a v lovely cathedral. He decided, when came to Durham, that he would what his architects could do on the s

Above: ②
View across the nave. These huge pillars, with incised decorations, afford vistas of great grandeur.

Right: ⑮
The Chapel of the Nine Altars. Loftiness and soaring lines are obtained in the chapel by sinking the floor below the level of the body of the church.

south and north transepts were finished. The north transept was covered with the present-day stone vaulting; the choir was also roofed in the same way, but its vaulting was changed later. The south transept then had a wooden ceiling. Two bays of the nave and aisles were completed and one bay of the triforium.

After Flambard's death in 1128 no bishop was appointed for five years and during that time the monks continued to build the nave and complete the aisles and finish the stone vaulting over them.

Right: (13)
The High Altar and Neville Screen, given by John, Lord Neville, about 1380. It is of Caen stone, wrought in London and brought by sea to Newcastle. It originally had 107 statues, all richly gilded and painted, the centre one representing Our Lady with St. Cuthbert and St. Oswald on either side. The large modern altar encloses a smaller Jacobean one still used occasionally.

where de Puiset's had failed. The original east end of the cathedral was in the form of an apse, but the masonry was then in a dangerous condition, because the appeal for funds which the bishop sent out represented the vaulting as liable to collapse at any minute. The essential repair work on the choir enabled the eastern end of it to be embellished in such a way as to blend with the style of the new building. The architect for this was Master Richard of Farnham, and though Bishop le Poore died before much could be done, the work went on under Prior Melsonby (1233–44). There were many priests in the monastery who, of course, needed to say Mass each day, so the new chapel was designed for nine altars and is referred to by that name.

Great periods of building alternated with periods of neglect, for when Prior John of Wessington, or Washington, was appointed in 1416, a vast amount of repair work was needed. He came from a family which, more than 300 years later, was to give America its first president. In the thirty years of his rule, he spent what was in those days the colossal sum of £7,881.8s.3d. on the cathedral and monastic buildings, as his accounts, which are still retained among the cathedral muniments, show. But even then he does not seem to have been able to repair the Bell Tower adequately. It was built originally in 1262, but was set on fire by lightning on the eve of Corpus Christi, 1429. It was patched up, but remained in a dangerous state until it was entirely rebuilt by Bishop Lawrence Booth. This was the last work done before the Reformation.

We possess a unique account of the appearance and day-to-day life of t[ ] great church at the end of the Mid[ ] Ages in a book referred to as the *Rites [of] Durham*. First published in 1672, it [is] believed to have been written in 1593 [by] one who had belonged to the monast[ery] in his youth. He either had a phe[no]menal memory or, possibly, an earl[y] manuscript account to guide him; for [he] dwells with loving delight on all t[he] minutiae of the building and its da[ily] routine. Take for example, his descr[ip]tion of the Jesus Altar, which sto[od] between the last two pillars at the e[ast] end of the nave before the lantern. T[he] wall on each side and the reredos behi[nd] it carried the story of Our Lord's passi[on] and of the twelve Apostles, carved [in] stone. Above it: "From pillar to pi[llar] was set up a border very artificia[lly] wrought in stone with marvellous fi[ne] colours, very curiously, and excellent[ly] finely gilt with branches and flowers, [the] more that a man did look at it the m[ore] desires he had, and the greater was [his] affection, to behold it." Above all: "[did] stand the most goodly and famous ro[od] that was in all this land, with the pictu[re] of Mary on the one side and the pictur[e of] John on the other, with two splendid a[nd] glistering Archangels, one on the [one] side of Mary and the other on the ot[her] side of John. So what for the fairness [of] the wall, the stateliness of the pictur[es] and the livelihood of the painting, it w[as] thought to be one of the goodliest mo[nu]ments in the Church."

Time and again as the author ling[ers] over some detail of beauty which h[as] been destroyed, he says with mourn[ful] pride: "It was the goodliest in all t[he] land." He tells us how the church w[as] appointed for the various Feast Days, [the] daily routine of monastic life, who ra[ng] the bells and when; he tells us of [the] books, the singing, the ornaments, a[nd] every point of interest about his belo[ved] church.

"Grey Towers of Durham, Yet well I love thy mixed and massive piles, Half church of God, half castle 'gainst the Scot.'' Sir Walter Scott

May, 1541, Henry VIII reconstituted
e Cathedral, appointing a Dean, and
clve prebendaries (canons) in place of
e monks, and ordering that the church
elf should be known as the Cathedral
urch of Christ and Blessed Mary the
rgin. The last Prior, Hugh Whitehead,
came the first Dean and the life of the
hedral went on. For a time White-
ad and his companions were able to
eserve things much as they had been.
e library in particular was kept more
less intact, which accounts for the
alth of medieval books and manu-
ripts which Durham still possesses.
e worst destruction took place after
hitehead's death. His successor,
bert Horne, was a convinced reform-
but he only held the office two years
ore Queen Mary's accession forced
n to flee to the continent, but he was
alled by Queen Elizabeth and was
an for two more years before becom-
Bishop of Winchester. He smashed
a good deal, but it was his successor,
lliam Whittingham, who was Dean
sixteen years, who completed the
vastation. To us it all seems wanton
ndalism, but only those who have
ed through a similar upheaval can
derstand the passions which inspire
n to the strange things they do at
ch times. No doubt to many the des-
ction appeared to be necessary on
igious grounds.
By the time of Dean Hunt (1620–38)
e Laudian reaction had set in and
nt began to beautify the cathedral
ain. He was assisted by John Cosin,
n one of the Canons, and afterwards
hop of Durham, who is a disting-
hed figure even in the long list of
tinguished men who have held the
e. They replaced the old wooden altar,
ich had done duty since the Reforma-
n, with a marble one which is still in
sition, though covered with a larger
e of wood. With its furniture it was

supposed to have cost above £3,000.
They also undertook a good deal of
repair work, particularly on the great
clock in the south transept, and did
considerable repainting and regilding.
This, and Cosin's insistence on music
and more attention to ritual in the
church's services, was a proceeding
which aroused tremendous wrath in
Peter Smart, who held the 6th Canonry.

Left: ⑬
View from the High
Altar
Below: ⑫
The Bishop's Throne,
said to be the highest
in Christendom,
surmounts the tomb of
Bishop Hatfield
(Bishop of Durham
1318–33). He built it
as his own memorial.

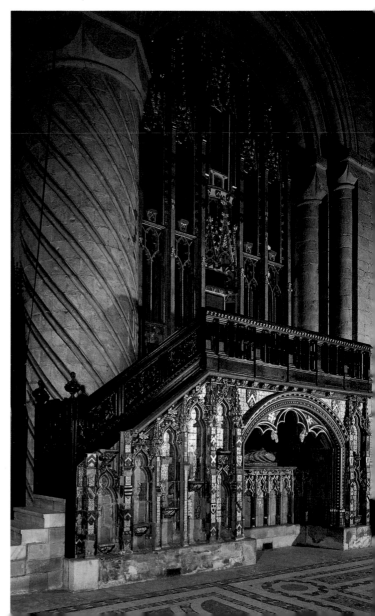

He was a man with a savage tongue and a vast stock of abuse, who seems to have cast himself for the part of the John Knox of Durham. He inveighed against Hunt and Cosin and all their works with unmeasured ferocity until be was deprived and imprisoned in 1628, but the Long Parliament restored him to his place again and he lived to give evidence at Laud's trial.

In 1650 what remained of medieval work inside the cathedral suffered still more. After the battle of Dunbar, on 3rd September in that year, Cromwell took 10,000 Scots prisoners and some 4,000 of these were shepherded down to Durham. There they were shut up in the cathedral, half-starved and exhausted with their march. No coals were allowed them, so they broke up all the woodwork of the choir stalls and everything else that they could lay their hands on which would burn, except the clock case, and used it for their fires. The clock is said to have been spared because it has a carving of the Scottish thistle on it, but no doubt men in prison found something which not only told the time but the phases of the moon and the seven stars a companionable thing to have, and perhaps left it alone on that account.

Great numbers of the prisoners died and were buried without much ceremony. Their jailer not only robbed the poor wretches of everything that he could get from them, but stole the brass lectern, shaped like a pelican, which was one of the few remaining pieces of medieval furniture, and sold it for his own profit.

Towards the end of his time, Cromwell planned to use the cathedral revenues for the foundation of a university in Durham, but the Charter was only just issued when he died and things stood still until the Restoration, when Church and King received their own again and John Cosin returned as bishop. There

was much to be done in the Diocese, b he did not neglect the cathedral on th account. He provided the choir sta now in position, the font and font cov (to the east of which is a bar of Froster. marble let into the floor, marking t extreme eastern limit to which wom were allowed to go in monastic time the litany desk and the faldstools, t small desks from which the litany w said, now in the sanctuary, and a gr carved oak screen carrying an organ, take the place of the stone screen whi had stood at the entry to the choir former days. His architect is said to ha been James Clement, who died in 16 and is buried in St. Oswald's churchya The Dean, John Sudbury, began to bu a library on what remained of the wa of the old refectory, but he died before was finished.

After that was completed there w little alteration anywhere for the n 100 years. The Deans were genera men of good family who had oth preferment in the south, where th liked to spend a great deal of their tir There were twelve prebendaries w were sometimes able, but always fluential men, for the cathedral w wealthy and its golden stalls were mu sought after. Those who held the usually stayed in Durham long enou to fulfil the statutory requirements a then departed to look after their oth interests. In 1777 the cathedral arc tect, Mr John Wooler, reported that t building was in an alarming state. the south side a crack in the vaulting r the whole length of the nave from east west. The wall on the cloister side w bulging outward and the stonewo everywhere was so badly eroded th water was seeping in. To remedy this suggested that the exterior should chipped away to the depth of four of i inches. All the towers and the pinnac needed urgent attention and the roo

above the north door, where watchm
had waited to receive fugitives, w
collapsing and should be pulled dov
The work was put in hand under
George Nicholson, Wooler's assista
who had just built Prebend's Bri
across the Wear for the Dean and Ch
ter. In the course of it much of
exterior decoration disappeared and
round window in the Nine Altars, wh
was to have been restored on its origi
plan, was altered to suit the fancy of
mason who did the work. James Wyat
often blamed for this destruction bu
was begun seventeen years before
appeared in Durham. When he did co
he left his mark. On his advice half
monastic chapter house was pul
down and a comfortable vestry made
of the remainder.

In 1840 drastic alterations to
cathedral began again and continued
over thirty years. The idea was to oj
up everything. The 17th-century org
screen, which separated the choir fr
the nave, was taken down, and in or
to get a longer vista still, the great do
at the west end, which Cardinal Lang
had blocked up with masonry, w
opened again so that there was
unimpeded view from the back of
Galilee Chapel right up to the High Al
But it proved to be a disappointm
after all. The great doors were clo
again; Langley's Altar which had st
behind them in the Galilee, and had be
destroyed in the search for vistas, w
replaced with a modern one. Up in
Chapel of the Nine Altars the woodw
round St. Cuthbert's shrine was tal
down in order to afford a view of the b
of the Neville Screen. Happily, much
found a home in the university libra
and has now been replaced with s
ficient new work to make it comple
The visitor can judge for himself if it is
poor a thing as it was said to b
hundred years ago.

About the same time, the clock in the
[sou]th transept, which belonged to
[Pri]or Castell's time (1494–1519) was
[tho]ught to be too grotesque for a sacred
[bui]lding, so the case (which had with-
[sto]od the ravages of Cromwell's prison-
[ers] after the Battle of Dunbar) was
[dis]mantled and the face of the clock itself
[set] in the wall of the transept. Many
[win]dows in the nave were altered and a
[num]ber filled with stained glass. Con-
[side]ring how poor Victorian glass often
[is,] much of what was put in then is
[sur]risingly good. The cloisters were re-
[pair]ed and the south end of the Monks'
[Dor]mitory, which had been used as a
[dw]elling-house for some time, was
[clea]red, so that the whole of that mag-
[nifi]cent room could be seen once more in
[its] original proportions. Dean Sudbury's
[libr]ary in the refectory was restored. The
[inc]ongruous plate glass windows which
[wer]e then put in have recently been
[repl]aced by leaded lights. A good deal of
[wor]k was done on the central tower
[und]er the direction of Sir Gilbert Scott.
[The] cement, which a previous architect
[had] plastered all over its exterior, was
[scr]aped off and part of the surface re-
[new]ed. Twenty-seven of the statues were
[rep]laced in their niches and thirteen new
[one]s added. The outline of the tower was
[thu]s considerably altered.

[R]emoving the organ screen had not
[bee]n as successful in improving the
[bea]uty of the cathedral as had been
[hop]ed. Something was obviously needed
[to b]reak the long line of vision from the
[wes]t to the east end; so between 1870
[and] 1876 Sir Gilbert Scott put up the
[mar]ble and alabaster screen which still
[stan]ds at the entrance to the choir, and
[the] ornate pulpit alongside it. The best
[tha]t can be said of them is that they
[mig]ht not look so bad anywhere else. At
[the] same time the plaster and whitewash
[whi]ch had covered all the inside walls of
[the] cathedral was cleaned off and it was

possible to see what they really looked
like once more. The choir and the sanctuary were refloored with marble, and
Hunt's altar covered with the larger one
which is, however, taken away each
year in Holy Week and Advent, so that
the Jacobean altar can be seen in something like its original array. In 1895 the
Chapter House was restored in memory
of Bishop Lightfoot.

Above: (2)
The font and the cover
were provided in the
last half of the 17th-
century by Bishop
John Cosin.

Left: (9)
The Clock, south
transept. The case is
late 15th century. The
dials and works were
renewed in 1632.

The Treasury and Monks' Dormitory

The Cathedral Treasury is a display of valuable and beautiful objects that are a guide through the nine hundred years of the cathedral's history. Here are to be found the relics of St. Cuthbert (including the coffin that brought his body to Durham in 995), fine altar plate, richly illustrated manuscripts, bishops' rings and seals, embroidered copes. All have played their part in the cathedral's life.

The Monks' Dormitory, situated above the Treasury, is now a library. It is regularly open to the public between Easter and the end of September.

Below:
The Monks' Dormi[tory]
Begun in 1398 and
finished in 1404, th[e]
Monks' Dormitory [was]
at that time divided
into small cubicles. [It]
still retains its origi[nal]
roof timbers.

Left:
A certified copy of [the]
1662 Prayer Book [with]
the Great Seal of
Charles II.

Right (above):
Standing paten and
cover (17th-centur[y])
bearing Bishop Co[sin's]
coat-of-arms.

Right (centre):
The hood of a cope
made for the visit o[f]
Charles I, showing
David with the hea[d of]
Goliath.

Right (below):
Title page of St. Jo[hn's]
Gospel, from the
Durham Gospels. T[he]
7th-century scribe [was]
clearly a master of
handwriting and
illumination.

Left: (19)
The Great Seal of
Bishop Hatfield, 1378.

Below: (10)
A capital letter from
Hugh de Puiset's
Bible.

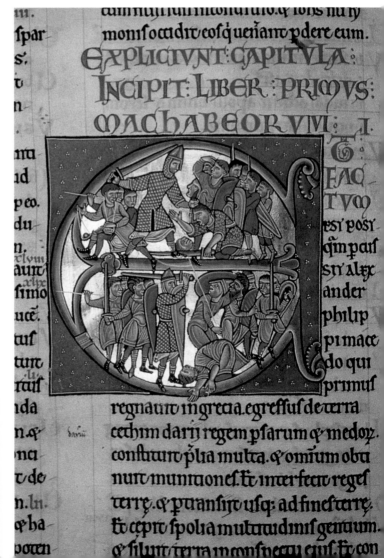

The Cathedral and the Community

"A 'community of care-takers', we ... encourage learning and the arts." The words of the Dean today would have been just as true uttered at almost any time during the cathedral's history. It had a strong teaching tradition even before the foundation of the University of Durham. By both its Charter and its Statutes, the cathedral had always been charged with the duty of educating youth and, in pursuance of this duty, had maintained a Public School; but with the growth of industry and the consequent rise in population, the need for a university in the north of England became ever more acute. In the new age that began with the agitation for the Reform Act, it was imperative that some-

thing should be done. In August 1831, Dr Jenkinson, who was both Dean of Durham and Bishop of St. David's, wrote to some members of the Chapter suggesting that they should consider a large scheme of education to be connected with the cathedral. By September of the same year the Chapter had a plan ready for the establishment of a university. The Bishop of Durham, William van Mildert, joined in with gifts of money and land, and ultimately handed over his castle in Durham as a home for the new college. The Dean and Chapter gave property to the value of £3,000 a year, and on 4th July 1832, less than a year after the scheme had been mooted, an Act of Parliament establishing the new univer-

Left:
The Miners' Memo[...]
The woodwork is
largely Spanish of [...]
17th century, but t[...]
foliage and cherub[...]
are English Jacobe[...]

received the Royal Assent. The
lve Canonries were reduced to five,
of them to be occupied by professors
he university. One canon professor
exists. For a long time the Dean was
the Warden of the University.

he cathedral touches every part of
life of the city and county of Durham.
ing has for long been one of the basic
ustries of the area and the cathedral's
ociation with it has always been
e, as witnessed by the 1947 Miners'
norial. The armed forces, too, are
represented at special services and,
r the First World War, the Dean and
pter dedicated a chapel to com-
norate the service of the 37 bat-
ons of the Durham Light Infantry in
parts of the world. The ensign worn
HMS Invincible during the Falklands
r is now hung in the south transept.

ver the past 50 years the work of
servation and renewal of the inside of
cathedral has continued and new
ks of art as well as fresh examples of
tsmen's skills have added to its
uty. Bishop Hatfield's tomb has been
ainted and gilded and a tester de-
ed by Sir Ninian Comper hung over
Cuthbert's tomb. The Gregory Chapel
a new altar designed by George Pace,
a new oak lectern has replaced the
e brass one designed by Gilbert Scott,
ch has itself been restored. Stained
s by Hugh Easton, Alan Younger
Mark Angus has been placed in
dows in the Chapter House, nave
Galilee Chapel, where there is some
lettering in a memorial by Bede's
b. Renate Melinsky has designed and
e a new set of Cathedral copes.
anie Sproat has designed and made
new chalices and patens in silver
gold. The timeless arts of stone
onry and carpentry are still pract-
by the cathedral craftsmen, refurb-
ng and repairing to keep the fabric of
cathedral in good order. It costs

Left: ⑧
The Barrington Statue.
Bishop Barrington was
a friend of the
evangelicals, a great
philanthropist and
interested in farming.
His statue is an
excellent example of
Chantrey's work.

Left: ⑮
The memorial to
Bishop William Van
Mildert (1765–1836).
He was the last Prince
Bishop, and was co-
founder, with the Dean
and Chapter, of
Durham University.

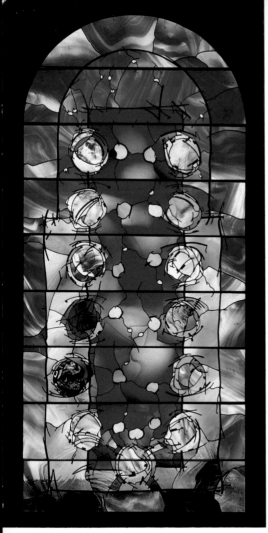

£500,000 a year to pay for the eighty or so full and part-time staff needed to repair the buildings and all the materials and equipment they need; to provide all that is required for the music and singing of the services; to cover the cost of the cleaning, heating and lighting; to employ gardeners, administrative staff and the clergy, the Dean and Canons, who are ultimately responsible for taking care of this House of God.

In 1987 Durham Cathedral and Castle were designated a World Heritage Site of historical and architectural interest, deserving practical support and protection. The Norman architects and builders had broken new ground with the high-level rib vaulting, and Durham Cathedral remains one of the greatest achievements of Norman and Romanesque architecture.

For further information and background on the Cathedral, its life and history, visitors are recommended to visit the audio-visual display in the Prior's Hall Undercroft.

Left:
"Daily Bread", the stained-glass wind in the north nave a designed by Mark Angus. It was dona in 1984 by the Dur branch of Marks an Spencer to commemorate the centenary of the fir

Below:
Durham Cathedral Castle, designated World Heritage Site

Opposite:
The two towers, 14 feet high, add mass dignity to the west front. The cloisters were heavily restor in 1827, and lost m of their original character.

Opposite (inset):
A young stonemas carrying on a centuries-old tradit in the cathedral workshop.

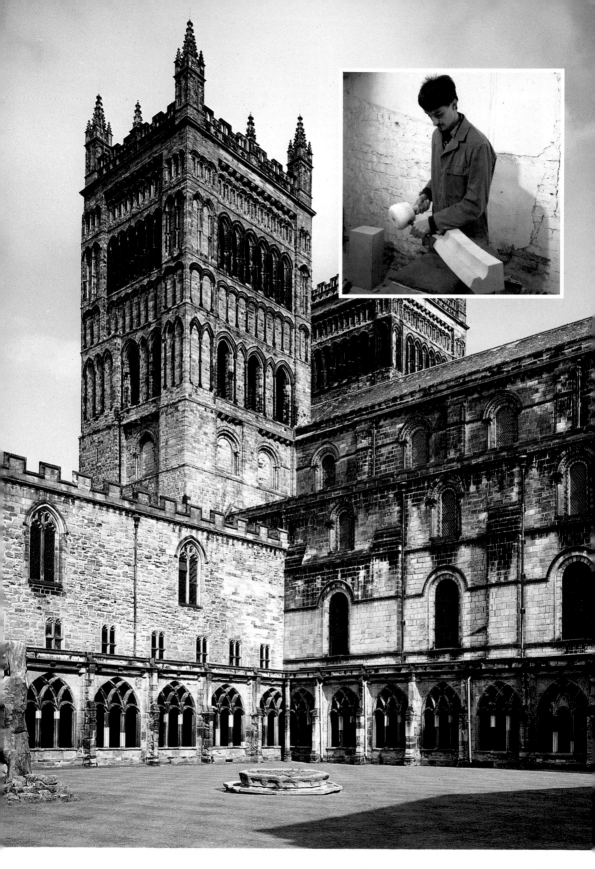

The Cathedral is a
living place. Here,
packed with peopl
the Christmas caro
service is just one
example of the
crowded special
services held each
for the parishes of
Durham Diocese, f
the university, the
armed forces, the
courts and the min